NOTES FROM THE WARD

STEFFI TAD-Y

Gordon Hill Press
Guelph, Ontario

Edited by Shane Neilson
Book design by Jeremy Luke Hill and Steffi Tad-y
Proofread by Mary Hamilton
Set in Linux Libertine and Swiss 721 Condensed
Printed on Mohawk Via Felt
Printed and bound by Arkay Design & Print

LIBRARY AND ARCHIVES CANADA CATALOGUING IN PUBLICATION

Title: Notes from the ward / Steffi Tad-y.
Names: Tad-y, Steffi, author.
Identifiers: Canadiana (print) 20250221063 | Canadiana (ebook) 20250226014 | ISBN 9781774221679 (softcover) | ISBN 9781774221693 (HTML) | ISBN 9781774221686 (PDF)
Subjects: LCGFT: Poetry.
Classification: LCC PS8639.A24 N68 2025 | DDC C811/.6—dc23

ONTARIO ARTS COUNCIL
CONSEIL DES ARTS DE L'ONTARIO
an Ontario government agency
un organisme du gouvernement de l'Ontario
Canada Council for the Arts | Conseil des arts du Canada
ONTARIO CREATES | ONTARIO CRÉATIF

Gordon Hill Press gratefully acknowledges the support of the Canada Council for the Arts, the Ontario Arts Council, and the Ontario Book Publishing Tax Credit.

Gordon Hill Press respectfully acknowledges the ancestral homelands of the Attawandaron, Anishinaabe, Haudenosaunee, and Métis Peoples, and recognizes that we are situated on Treaty 3 territory, the traditional territory of Mississaugas of the Credit First Nation.

Gordon Hill Press also recognizes and supports the diverse persons who make up its community, regardless of race, age, culture, ability, ethnicity, nationality, gender identity and expression, sexual orientation, marital status, religious affiliation, and socioeconomic status.

Gordon Hill Press
130 Dublin Street North
Guelph, Ontario, Canada
N1H 4N4
www.gordonhillpress.com

Table of Contents

Episode

Illness, unpinnable.
In my head, I was mother

to a god,
god to a mother.

Body belonging to men.
The doctor reported

distorted, disheveled.
Desire taken to extremes.

In the lunchroom,
my mother combs my hair,

touches my dry hands.
My father opens the Tupperware

of fish stew & cake.
In an instant, I am

the days I covet,
the child in my dreams.

But what matters now is not a question of profitability, not a question increased productivity, not a question of production rates. Not, it is not a question of back to nature. It is the very basic question of not dragging man in directions which mutilate him, of not imposing on his brain tempos that rapidly obliterate and unhinge it.
— Frantz Fanon

I would not have survived if not for the care of others.
— Angeli Lacson

You Who The Earth Was For

After Jean Valentine

You fleeing war, carrying a rooster with your shaky hand.
You trained to pummel, never the first to wince or flinch.

You who plant their sadness into dirt.
You whose questions have no gentle answers.

You who cook too close to the stove.
You at the table, missing the one.

You whose loss comes with wordlessness.
You beside the rubble, out to build again.

You in the backseat being loved.
You running towards water.

The Day I Lose My Job

My neighbour whose name I don't know holds the door for me as I throw out the evening's garbage bags. By the green bin, squirrels leave a trail of caramel popcorn that looks like confetti in the dark. The television show I watch ends with a thank you to all who made it possible. The last episode closes with a small ship sailing out of a child's bedroom. The moon is full and I sleep to the sound of the ocean glowing on my laptop screen. Underneath the floorboards, a family rocks to their own karaoke. I breathe in and out with lungs the shape of trees

Postscript to Mania

After Shira Erlichman

I bought rainbow scarves   & pastel-coloured napkins   then begged

near turnstiles & bus stops   for silver ducats   because there was hunger

& I could no longer afford   a slice of pizza.   Up high & bereft   of self-seeing

until someone came with gifts.   I remember chiffon cake   with the words

"Steffi, see you soon"   in midnight blue icing   for the stray dog in me,

friend a member of me.

Notes from the Ward #1

First bits of pink in the cramped winter grey.

Three letters of recommendation.

Congratulations! You have the job.

Cheese without the threat of flatulence.

Mauve and seafoam socks for my birthday.

Meat & berries & kin.

Softness as a kind of spine.

Sleep & shelter.

Light to prune the overgrowth.

Photographs of my young mother.

Spring

I laughed & even the flowers
thought I was too loud.

Out with my brother
whom I have not seen in years,

our walks are in technicolour.

Every neon sign a delirious
invitation for a pun or a joke.

Two of us, the world quaking.

Heads & Tails

Simplicity gets to you.

The velvet nose of pups,

or a child half her uncle's size

singing to sunflowers.

One day in a bog close to Minoru,

paw & foot astride

stopped to look at sky.

Contrails like giant fishbones

caught in a cloud's throat.

A salamander pocketed for safety.

A whiff of fir & pine

& the brittle self-forgets.

A small woman, snow-haired

with eyes a shade of Pacific

swaying to the Bee Gees,

staying alive.

Notes from the Ward #2

I'm not anybody's widow or orphan,
but my friends & I (a handful) tried to jump.

But M, she told me, She is | She continues
though the past. By the green-tiled hallway

I planted my hands on the ground

& for a few brave seconds
turned my body upside down.

I felt blood travel
from my feet to my head.

I found my grandmother there
& in Nueva Ecija.

Her blade work with rice fields
& fireflies, witnesses to her love.

Wake

The sky yet to fume
& suffuse the nation with sweat –

where we were, tamarind
& steady wind by the window.

Each with a pillows to chest,
I patted your fifty-seven-year-old

hair, more salt than silk.
That Sunday, we did not talk

about which ball player choked,
who was favoured to win,

or some lining in the cloud.
From the quiet we heard

the makings of Mom preparing
food for the funeral.

We parted curtains,
faced the generous window.

Leaves lend heft
to the word *rustle.*

Leaves with so much green to give,
trees sounding like the rain.

Live your beautiful life, baby

Undcr my umbrella
on a rainy day

I pass a boy
by himself

on the field
young enough

to be my son,
probably in fifth grade

his face
a cloud of calm

in the cold
before he kicks the ball

over the crossbar
& in between

the uprights
to score a three.

I try not to
crinkle my face

like confetti.
How badly

the inner dad
or big sister

in me wants
to yell yes

my guy, that kick
was the jam

such good music
with his feet.

Just a little bit
over a decade old,

gathering composure
on the ground,

his breath
solemn & deliberate.

With the Bee Gees
still in my ears,

("How Deep is Your Love"
this time)

I looked away,
afraid my gaze

might knave
his shot.

Still I held him
in my spirit,

this boy,
a reminder

of another,
the one, through

the many red
& ruminant seasons

of fall, grew
& grew with me.

Notes from the Ward #3

After Ocean Vuong's "Reasons for Staying"

Think of the next thirty years, mother asked.

The magnolia tree at Oben Street still a pleasant memory.

Of the book, black with deep blue letters, music despite my lack
of understanding.

My legs on my grandma's lap.

Hands making & making.

My father hauling a family mattress in the rain.

The A/C wind on my face & the chatter of young ones behind.

Seconds of optimism.

The window bright.

Noli Me Tangere

When I was in high school, I splattered Pond's whitening cream on my face. But I'd miss the neck. In *Noli Me Tangere*, Padre Damaso loses it at the bougie banquet when all he got apart from a bony wing was a bare neck in his bowl of chicken tinola. Since then, I wear my neck proudly. This thick and short stump. A brown bridge & vessel to a brown river, brown house, brown land. It is a five-hundred-year challenge not to hurl an invective at friars for the horrors they hid under the table and under their robes, but my guidance counsellor had a poster up her wall that asked, "What is the opposite of prison?" I do not know but I will begin by praising. I will kneel on the hard ground and for every bead I clutch, I will say amen to every brown bridge, brown vessel, brown river, brown house, brown land that birthed and continues to birth my brown, brown life possible & this time, I will not look up nor bow my head down. Remember, I missed the neck.

Notes from the Ward #4

Getting the sense
I should lessen

for people's comfort,
all closing

of myself falls
when with our backs

to the sun
T sees me questioning

my hands,
how to make it fly.

Trust a bird
if you see one,

even when
it is a shadow.

Alitaptap

Every field,
a father.

Every fire,
a missing son.

Thousands now,
a barricade.

Mangroves
rooted in coral
mud & rock.

Once near a row
of sugar cane

on a road slicing
between carnival

& cemetery
cavities

to the chest,
I am

my mother
& her mother's prayer.

Notes from the Ward #5

When I woke midafternoon
        from the hospital bed

remembering families
        I am no longer part of

I ran to the hallway
        to our strip, our block,

our *neighbourhood*
        as T calls us

by the only window
        where we could see

the city outside.
        We sat in a circle

passing time
        in our paisley gowns

& blue chairs
        like ladies out in the field

or the church,
        witnesses to one another's

unsaid pressures,
        painting each other's nails.

Walking Around Poland St.

I forget
the world is holy

an elder
asked

by a boy
in his teens

underneath
the powder blue

streamers
if she's taken

her medicine.
They laugh.

Touch
elbows.

Speak of
metformin

& pressures
of the blood.

Just yesterday,
on the hottest

day of the year,
someone's sister

slid a towel
on their back.

22 It is not
yet Christmas

which starts in
September here

but a sea
of lights

dot the evening sky.
Children scream

& yet it as though
they are singing.

Yesterday, I walked in
on my dad saying

his morning prayers
inside the chapel

with a blue sign:
Adoration ongoing.

I adore the kid
skipping

with a bucket
of fried chicken

before the six p.m.
church bells ring.

His neighbour
leaves a small

sieve of honey
for butterflies

about to fly
on their own.

It is clear
how I want

to be saved
by what I can

catch
with my eye.

Tubthumping at Queens

Tremor makes a house

        out of my hands.

Notice the birds of paradise,

        peach & sunrise

inside the atrium

        of a music building.

Last week, my brother finished school

        &, facing all of us, blooms.

Doors opened & families of graduates

        entered, taking photographs

(writing with light)

        their beloved in toga & tassel

wreathed with flowers & clouds.

        A cap that moved my eye

had the word *courage*

        sewn on its black square.

I roam its shape.

Trace how *cour* is

a letter away from *coeur*

meaning *heart*

which in my hustle

& vocabulary remained

a young boy boxing,

inching heaven

after being knocked out.

Notes from the Ward #6

Michael Jackson's "I'll be there"
plays from the nurses' station.

K blows Mamita a kiss & Mamita kisses back.
R cranks Souljaboy like it's 2006.

Sunlight from giant windows,
G raps, searching truth through sound.

Pingpong from the therapy room.
Here we raise our hands

& wave to YouTube music across decades.
My turn, I choose Biggie.

Paradise until someone screams
for a sandwich, mustard packets

without a sliver of glass,
*you pieces of sh*t.*

The shouting begins. Nurse C says,
Don't take anything personally in here.

G continues to rap. *I thrive in repetition*
but we've dwelt too long on this mount.

Asked to make this our goal:
never come back.

I stay in the hallway,
tracing lines on the floor.

Sesamoids.

Mangroves

My doctor says I'm a little manic. Instead of waves or the bellows of breath, I think of mangroves by the sea. How their roots are home to the fish & crabs in need of refuge. I nestle there.

*

Back in the truck with Dad & Uncle, I tell them how the trees are skin & sanctuary to the coast, protection against the onslaught of storms.

My father places his hand on the headrest of my uncle in the driver seat and says, Families can be mangroves too.

*

By the shore, a woman talks to us.

Dako gid ang bulig 'sang mangroves.
    The mangroves were a big help.
'Kay sang Yolanda, ang mga bahay gatumba.
    During the storm Yolanda, houses fell.
Ang bangka gaguba.
    Boats were destroyed.
Tatlo ka beses na kami kalipat.
    We moved three times.
Kung kusog ang alon.
    When the wave surged.
Kung kusog ang hangin.
    When the winds hurtled.
Ara da sila.
    They were there.

*

A crowd of children play under the *bakhawan*. Intertwined trees form a small, open dome. Recovery militates. I can soften into the earth.

Notes from the Ward #7

While the Raptors
slugged it out

with the Warriors
at Air Canada Stadium,

which I watched
from a grainy television

in Manila,
what I didn't see coming

was Fred VanVleet
elbowed

underneath the basket
blood like river

through his cheek.
The cameraman

zoomed to
the shiny hardwood floor

where he fell and where
we can see so clearly

his chipped tooth.
When Rilke said *keep going*

no feeling is final
terror or madness

keep going
I think about Fred

I think about his tooth
and how, if ever at all,

do we get to know
where we're headed

and if ever at all
do we get to know

through the dirt & effort
of our dreaming

do we land.

Where We Meet

On the train line from Richmond-Brighouse to City Centre, an elderly woman takes out a miniature tub of petroleum jelly from her purse and lines her fingers with grease, massages the space between her thumb and index, then the middle finger, the pinky. Why must I stare, memorizing every detail—I'll need them at some point? Like that time I saw two women who rushed toward each other in the middle of a packed moviehouse and hugged. During the pandemic, I saw my mother and her mother everywhere.

After A Vertical Interrogation of Strangers

Kamay sa bulsa, anong dala-dala?
Hand in pocket, what do you carry?

Namako na ang iyong mga kuko?
Have your nails caused harm?

Kailangan mo ba ng pera?
Do you need money?

Ano ang huni ng iyong panaginip?
What is the shape of your dream?

Notes from the Ward #8

I am envious of J who takes care of us. With his green pen & brown clipboard checking how we are. His steady chair below the silver clock where he listens to each of our stories, our requests for more milk, sandwiches, or tissue rolls. When I ask him why he is so kind to us, he says, *It is my job to treat you right.* I want that for myself too—a purpose unstaggered. Behind him was a painting of birds, and a bird above it.

I Hid in the Possibility of an Aurora Borealis Sky

"You have a gift for dark things."
no comeback for this   in years
by the Spanish Banks   on the lookout
for a sliver of the North   my heart
a fish that slips   from my hands
& bellyflops into the ocean   at night time
where it loves   being a muscle
pressed so close to the core
of the Earth it shines

Cento: This body, this mind

every part to the tiniest hair
down in a narrow boat
how you learned to love me in my sleep

contaminates every river it has known
sweat gladly in time
falling to the ground

ready to push
facing east
little book on which I in my hunger wrote

unbodied by heat
island cast in the windcombed sea
with narcotic holiness

lens I can look through with my mind
like fire or sleet
fallen still

cosmos flowers
big with ribs
before me at all times

strummed & stamped
midnight & fireworks
simply gave out

divided into zones
aches in small lights
couldn't control

underground sea of letters
watery and adjusting
distant and forbidden sunken sun

dressed for summer
a signal of meat thus of hunger
indeterminate

river that shapes the landscape
waking reach
only trying

cannot be blamed to be in 5 places at once
above the slatted fields
still insists

multimillion
slow and out of focus
the impossibility

an umbrella
a finite room
bright blue pool

the glue &
each puzzle piece chewed
an embarrassing relative

lightheaded and hawked
borderline with the universe
hungering after likenesses

a float house
yields the floor
empties, turns to you

must tread slow
sees the garden in the green
where another forest lived

each wrinkle intact
crossing the sky
buoyant than I realize

needs reminding
ancient sound fills every sidewalk
why don't you stay

Notes from the Ward #9

That a plane
        can be a shell

or an earring
        grazing my earlobe.

As I look up
        at a cloudless sky,

I feel heat
        in my body.

How M just walked
        with it, asked

what was I thinking
        after him saying,

You must
        find someone

who understands,
        it takes years.

When I asked him
        the same question,

he said
        quietly,

You, I am
        thinking
about you.

After Confinement

I.

As I pass by a repair shop tending to all parts of a washing machine, electric fan & air conditioner, I play East Forest's "Limitations" on my phone. I burrow into the piano keys, their music gliding towards my ear.

How to say I cannot think well.

My brain sick for months.

Searching for cadence & cohesiveness.

My I not a machine nor music however much I bargain or command.

In the realm of rupture & dream, I am purposeful. I move from
one whirr to the next with ease.
Efforts funnelled to keep a home going. Switch from on to off as
reliable as the grid powering the city. Into many nights, all
the stories in me buck & I keep on breaking.

How do I extend myself some love?

When do I rest into the we?

III.

We take turns

singing

our stories

our mountains

We practice

our dance moves

chicken wings + pizza

= not all is lost

We laugh

& castigation hums to a close

Notes from the Ward #10

For Aracelis Girmay

Remembering love
I'm no longer with,

I turn to the música
of a poet who over

the years has carried
water for a wound,

my wound,
so open fruit flies

congregate
& make of it

a landing place.

Her cadence I clutch
like a rosary

at night.

How she teaches me to
lift my sorrow out of sorrow.

despite the hard
& violet streaks

found in my hands.

Flags or No, There is No "Nothing There"

After Marc Perez

On Monday mornings
I placed my right hand over my [ ]

to declare [ ] for a nation
where mothers, thousands every day

must leave [ ] so their children
may live. At night even the wind is a mother.

El Niño. La Niña.

Shelters

[

]
As she storms –

[

]

eldest daughter of an eldest daughter
of an eldest daughter of an eldest daughter
crossing International Date Line, a report:

Nervous system [ ] born in a warming south

[

[   ] racking up debt
to quell doubt

]

Signed, here [   ] above the equator

Dayo. Natututo palang
lumugar.

Dreaming of *Nanay.*

Notes from the Ward #11

From where I stand,
        above & afar, a police car

wheels through the street
        that matches* my throat.

It is a life-long practice
        to abolish my inner cop.

She who deserves
        my care despite

the unwise
        [

...]

& unloving

        [

...]

        she commits.

A Coffee Ad Asked, "What Gets You Up in the Morning?"

the desired habit   was to roll out of bed   like a lemon

bright, ripe   and full of purpose,   tipped into a glass

of clean water   not like this   stale milk   rotting tooth

throat easily locked   my father messaged   an overflow

of mangoes   in millions   leaving home   in kahas

I Had Forgotten About The Clapping

When I was four,
outside the mansion
of a chocolate conglomerate
my mother cooked
& catered for, I was

given a red helium balloon
I held with one hand
while the other clasped
a juice box. I was about
to slide into her car when

I released my grip
from the balloon,
which in this re-telling,
now hovers
above a silver roof. Before

I can even gasp
& make my words
ask for help,
the waiter beside me

had already
clapped constantly
for the balloon
to get down.
But then my palm
would open again

& this time
the balloon
flew too high & fast.

Snot on my jumper
& in the backseat,
my body played out
the night like
a crushed juice box.

Groundhog Day in Blue and Yellow

There was no singing, no singing at all

Inside a bungalow / my bed wet
a pungent patch / pool of green

Within each slant, something silent screams
and to hear the lullaby, I cupped my hands
over unsevered ears

Sleepwalking since I was eight, risk
factors were key

The poems were rooms but their doors
were shut

I did not know samskara
nor prefiguring

Through the years, a spectrum
shrivelled disks to starry nights

Theo who loved him

Notes from the Ward #12

The night before I leave, I am glued to the bed. My blue sweater & green shorts remind me I am part of this Earth. I could not stop the past from murmuring. She pulls a chair towards where I am. I look for the stamina not to fragment. I practice my apologies. Write them on my notebook:

I'm sorry
I was out of line
I snapped
I should've stopped

At Valley Stream

Running after my nephew,

I spot his tonsils,   red & laughing

as if a wound never happened.

From the ward, I am told I must say what I think.

Today the ocean is not   a limit nor a consolation,

but a beginning   of a strawberry day,

ensconced in green   & younger kin

held & holding.

Proposition

When my grandmother reads the news that volcanoes,
    Mayon & Taal, were threatening to blow,

I tried not to make the comparison,
    shun the easy link to my mind yet there I was.

Why can't the language I tread lead me closer
    to horses evacuating before the eruption?

How they fled from their deaths.
    Or the flowers that grew from lahar,

lava that cooled & once warmed the land.

Hold on

Everyone has something.

This is yours.

The trees & their rings are with you.

The blade that in time

turned into a flock of birds.

The kites at dusk

like children in the sky.

Not everything

is marred by violence.

Roots are everywhere.

Naming what we love.

Meeting our breath.

Song greening song.

Blue and Yellow Road

With gratitude to Wayde Compton

At the end of the hallway, where we get to face the only section of the ward with windows that showed us the rest of where we were in the world—the traffic lights, kids off the school bus, the convenience stores, police stations, and parking lots—L takes my black composition notebooks P, one of the therapists, gave me.

Let me write you a business plan, L says.

She has seen me in warrior I and II poses on the floor and we've had enough time together for me to spill, despite all my defenses, that I would like to teach yoga but I am scared because how can I expect people to trust me with their bodies when I can't even trust my own mind.

A couple of years later, after this encounter with L who I will never see again because I didn't even get to know her real name, I was looking at trees being blown steadily by the wind. My mind, which has never been good at sequencing, jumped to Baron Geisler and Kanye West. I imagined sitting beside them by the shoreline, any shoreline.

I'd take (yes, take) a breath and for a few seconds, let the ocean be ocean.

When I feel like we're ready, I'd tell Geisler or West, without looking them in the eye which might threaten or confuse, I *know I'm not looking pretty good myself, but how are you really doing, brother?*

Acknowledgements

Angel Nafis, Shira Erlichman, Joanne Arnott, Oliver de la Paz, Rick Barot, Justyna Król, Marc Perez, Jody Chan, Karla Comanda, Chris Nazaire, Johna Baylon, Jeremiah Mari Carag, Erie Maestro, Phebe Ferrer, Alyssa De Jesus, Leanne Dunic, Shane Neilson, Jeremy Luke Hill, thank you.

The BC Arts Council for their financial assistance.

Reader, thank you.

About the Author

Born and raised in Manila, Philippines, Steffi Tad-y is a poet and writer based in the territories of the Musqueam, Squamish, and Tsleil-Waututh Nations, also known as Vancouver, British Columbia. Her chapbook of poems *Merienda* published by Rahila's Ghost Press was nominated for the 2021 bpNichol Chapbook Award. In 2022, she published her debut book of poetry *From the Shoreline* with Gordon Hill Press. Steffi's poems often reflect on kinship, diasporic geographies, and formations of the mind.